First World War
and Army of Occupation
War Diary
France, Belgium and Germany

2 DIVISION
1 Light Brigade
Headquarters,
King's Royal Rifle Corps 13th, 18th and 20th Battalions
3 April 1919 - 31 July 1919

WO95/1374/1-4

The Naval & Military Press Ltd
www.nmarchive.com
Published in association with The National Archives

Published by

The Naval & Military Press Ltd

Unit 10 Ridgewood Industrial Park,
Uckfield, East Sussex,
TN22 5QE England
Tel: +44 (0) 1825 749494

www.naval-military-press.com
www.nmarchive.com

This diary has been reprinted in facsimile from the original. Any imperfections are inevitably reproduced and the quality may fall short of modern type and cartographic standards.

© **Crown Copyright**
Images reproduced by permission of The National Archives, London, England, 2015.

Contents

Document type	Place/Title	Date From	Date To
Heading	WO95/1374/1		
Heading	BEF 2 Division HQ 1 Light Brigade 1919 April-1919 Jly		
War Diary	Dormagen	03/04/1919	23/05/1919
Miscellaneous	Special Order Appendix A	17/05/1919	17/05/1919
War Diary	Dormagen	02/06/1919	11/07/1919
War Diary	Solingen	21/07/1919	31/07/1919
Heading	WO95/1374/2		
Heading	2 Division 1 Light Brigade 13 K R R C 1919 Mar-1919 Oct		
Heading	War Diary For Month Of March Volume No.44		
War Diary	Jumet	01/03/1919	01/03/1919
War Diary	Oberaussem	02/03/1919	25/03/1919
War Diary	Dormagen	26/03/1919	31/03/1919
Miscellaneous	Statement Of Strength-March 1919		
War Diary	Dormagen	01/04/1919	30/05/1919
War Diary	Dormagen Germany	01/06/1919	11/07/1919
War Diary	Solingen	16/07/1919	29/10/1919
Heading	WO95/1374/3		
Heading	BEF 2 Division 1 Light Brigade 18 K R R C 1919 April-1919 Oct From 41 Div 122 Bde		
War Diary	Niederaussem Oberaussem	01/04/1919	07/04/1919
War Diary	Worringen	07/04/1919	16/06/1919
War Diary	Mulheim	17/06/1919	17/06/1919
War Diary	Marienburg	21/06/1919	30/06/1919
War Diary	Worringen	03/06/1919	16/06/1919
War Diary	Mulheim	17/06/1919	17/06/1919
War Diary	Marienburg	21/06/1919	30/06/1919
Miscellaneous	18th Bn. K.R.R.C. Move Order No.1	16/06/1919	16/06/1919
Miscellaneous	18th Bn. K.R.R.C.	17/06/1919	17/06/1919
Miscellaneous	18th Bn. K.R.R.C. Move Order No.2	20/06/1919	20/06/1919
Miscellaneous	18th Battn. King's Royal Rifle Corps Move Order No. 2 (a)	29/06/1919	29/06/1919
Miscellaneous	18th Battalion King's Royal Rifle Corps Move Order 3 (B)	30/06/1919	30/06/1919
War Diary	Marienburg	01/07/1919	01/07/1919
War Diary	Worringen	03/07/1919	11/07/1919
War Diary	Solingen	17/07/1919	31/07/1919
Miscellaneous	18th Battn. King's Royal Rifle Corps Move Order No. 3 (a)	29/06/1919	29/06/1919
Miscellaneous	18th Battalion King's Royal Rifle Corps Move Order No. 4 (b)	09/07/1919	09/07/1919
War Diary	Solingen	02/08/1919	28/08/1919
Miscellaneous	18th Battn. King's Royal Rifle Corps Defence Scheme	04/08/1919	04/08/1919
War Diary	Solingen	02/08/1919	18/10/1919
War Diary	Ohligs	22/10/1919	30/10/1919
War Diary	Solingen	02/10/1919	18/10/1919
War Diary	Ohligs	22/10/1919	30/10/1919
Miscellaneous	18th Bn. K.R.R.C. Move Order No. 6 (a)	21/10/1919	21/10/1919
Miscellaneous	O.C. 18th Bn. K.R.R.C.		

Miscellaneous	18th Battalion King's Royal Rifle Corps Action on Cut Break of Civil Disturbance	26/10/1919	26/10/1919
Heading	WO95/1374/4		
Heading	2 Div 1 Light Bde 20th Bn K.R.R.C. 1919 Feb-1919 Jly		
War Diary	Duren Germany	01/02/1919	06/04/1919
War Diary	Zons (Germany)	08/04/1919	17/05/1919
War Diary	Harff	19/05/1919	19/05/1919
War Diary	Zons	19/05/1919	30/05/1919
War Diary	Zons (Germany)	02/06/1919	11/07/1919
War Diary	Solingen	23/07/1919	31/07/1919

WO95/13744

BEF

2 (~~Light~~) DIVISION

HQ 1 LIGHT BRIGADE

1919 APRIL — 1919 JULY

Army Form C. 2118.

WAR DIARY
or
INTELLIGENCE SUMMARY.
(Erase heading not required).

Instructions regarding War Diaries and Intelligence Summaries are contained in F.S. Regs., Part II. and the Staff Manual respectively. Title pages will be prepared in manuscript.

18th Bde

Place	Date	Hour	Summary of Events and Information	Remarks and references to Appendices
DORMAGEN.	April 3rd.		The Divisional Commander Major-General Sir R.D. Whigham K.C.B. D.S.O. arrived and took over Command of the Light Division.	
	5th.		Division Commander visited the Brigade.	
	6th.		The Brigades of the Light Division were renamed as follows: 5th. Infty. Brigade, became 1st. Light Brigade, 99th. Infty. Bde. became 2nd. Light Brigade, 6th. Infty. Bde. became 3rd. Light Brigade at 6 a.m. this morning. The 20th. Bn. London Regt. left the Brigade to join the 2nd. Light Brigade at NETTESHEIM. The Bn. K.R.R.C. arrived during the afternoon to join the Brigade, taking over the quarters vacated by the 6th. Bn. London Regt. in ZONS and STURZELBURG. Strength of Battn. 26 Officers and 873 O.Rs. Battalion is commanded by Lieut-Colonel F.G. WILLAN C.M.G. D.S.O. The 5th. Bn. The King's Royal Rifle Corps. The 5th. Bn. Royal Irish Regt. arrived in the Brigade Area and took over the Guard found by 52nd. Bn. Rifle Brigade at LONGERICH. This Battalion is now Pioneer Battalion of the Light Division.	
	7th.		The 18th. Bn. K.R.R.C. arrived and were taken on the strength of this Brigade about noon today, strength 28 Officers and 498 O.Rs. Hd.Qrs. WORRINGEN, commanded by Lt.Col. Vernon D.S.O. The 52nd. Rifle Brigade entrained at WORRINGEN at 10-15 a.m. today to join the 3rd. Light Brigade at KONIGSHOVEN. Between 500 and 600 men from 53rd. Bn. K.R.R.C. joined the 20th. Bn. K.R.R.C. arriving at DORMAGEN at about noon today.	
	8th.		980 all ranks of 52nd. Bn. K.R.R.C. arrived at 10-17 a.m. for absorption by 18th. Bn. K.R.R.C. at WORRINGEN.	
	10th.		The Corps Commander visited 13th., 18th. and 20th. Bn. K.R.R.C.	
	11th.-24th.		Battalions carried out individual training.	
	24th.		The Divisional Commander inspected the 20th. Bn. K.R.R.Cn on parade at ZONS. Band of 1st. Bn. K.R.R.C. came to play to the Brigade for a week.	

Army Form C. 2118.

WAR DIARY
or
INTELLIGENCE SUMMARY.
(Erase heading not required.)

Place	Date	Hour	Summary of Events and Information	Remarks and references to Appendices
DORMAGEN	26th.		The Brigade Model Allotment was started at DORMAGEN under Lieut. RUSSEL with 4 Instructors and 12 Pupils.	
	26th.		A Launch was bought for the use of the Brigade.	

W. Horden.
Brigadier General,
Commdg. 1st. Light Brigade.

6/5/19

Army Form C. 2118.

WAR DIARY
or
INTELLIGENCE SUMMARY.
(Erase heading not required.)

1st. Light Brigade H.Q.

Instructions regarding War Diaries and Intelligence Summaries are contained in F. S. Regs., Part II. and the Staff Manual respectively. Title pages will be prepared in manuscript.

Place	Date	Hour	Summary of Events and Information	Remarks and references to Appendices
	3rd.		The 13th. & 18th. Battalions were inspected by the Divisional Commander, Major General Sir R.D. Whigham, K.C.B., D.S.O. at WORRINGEN. He expressed himself very pleased with the general turnout.	
	10th.		Brigade Motor Launch made its first trip.	
	17th.		The Commander-in-Chief, Sir William Robertson, G.C.B., K.C.V.O., D.S.O., A.D.C. inspected the Brigade (less 20th. Battalion whose billets at ZONS were inspected subsequently) at WORRINGEN. The Brigade subsequently marched past in fours. The C. in C. expressed himself very pleased with the whole parade. The Brigade Commander issued a special order (See Appendix A.)	
	23rd.		Orders were received for the Brigade to be prepared to move to the Cologne Area, in the event of a general move forward, being ordered. Move to be dependant on attitude of Germans to Peace terms.	
			Individual and platoon training were carried out throughout the month, simple tactical exercises with and without troops were carried out by all units at least twice a week. An elementary course of 50 rounds was fired by all ranks on Company miniature ranges.	
DORMAGEN.				
7/6/19.				

[signature]
Brigadier General,
Commanding, 1st. Light Brigade.

APPENDIX A.

1st. Light Brigade.

13th.K.R.R.C.
18th.K.R.R.C.
1st.L.T.M.B.
5th.F.A.

S P E C I A L   O R D E R.

 The Commander-in-Chief has directed me to convey to all ranks of the Brigade his appreciation of their excellent turn-out and smart soldier-like appearance on parade and during the march past to-day.

 He expressed himself well satisfied with all he saw and considered that great credit is due to all concerned.

 The Corps Commander also personally requested that his congratulations should be added to the Commander-in-Chief's appreciation.

****

 O.C.Units will cause this order to be made known to all under their command.

DORMAGEN.
17/5/19.

(Signed) G.V.Hordern, Brig.Gen.
Commanding.1st.Light Brigade.

1st.Light Brigade H.Qrs.

WAR DIARY or INTELLIGENCE SUMMARY.
(Erase heading not required.)

Army Form C. 2118.

Instructions regarding War Diaries and Intelligence Summaries are contained in F.S. Regs., Part II. and the Staff Manual respectively. Title pages will be prepared in manuscript.

Place	Date	Hour	Summary of Events and Information	Remarks and references to Appendices
DORMAGEN.	June 2nd.		A Brigade route march was carried out via DORMAGEN - HORREM - DELHOVEN.	
	3rd.	1000	Units in the Brigade paraded independently as strong as possible to celebrate the King's birthday. After the Royal Salute, three hearty cheers were given for His Majesty. The rest of the day was observed as a holiday.	
	13th.		The Brigade Commander in conjunction with the S.S.O. carried out one of their periodical inspection of Battalion Transports. Order of merit.- 18th.20th.& 13th.Battalions.	
	16th.		Orders received that moves in accordance with arrangements in the event of peace not being signed were to be put in force. (The Brigade under these orders had to move to COLOGNE to take over various guards) 18th Battalion K.R.R.C. were ordered to move to MULHEIM.	
	17th.		18th.Battalion moved across river to MULHEIM to take over temporarily guards of Southern Div.	
	18th.		The Corps Commander Lieut Gen. Sir A.J.Godley,K.C.B.,K.C.M.G. inspected the training of 20th. Battalion at ZONS who were doing platoon tactical schemes, also the barracks of 13th.Battalion at DORMAGEN.	
	21st.		18th.Battalion K.R.R.C. moved to MARINBURG. when it came under tactical command of 2nd Light Brigade.	
	28th.		Wire was received that Peace had been signed.	
	29th.		Orders received that all units were to return to their normal areas. 18th Battn K.R.R.C. to return to WORRINGEN on July 1st.	

July 14th.1919.

[signature] Capt.
Brigade Major,1st.Light Bde.

Army Form C. 2118.

WAR DIARY
or
INTELLIGENCE SUMMARY.
(Erase heading not required.)

1st. Light Brigade H.Q.

Instructions regarding War Diaries and Intelligence Summaries are contained in F. S. Regs., Part II. and the Staff Manual respectively. Title pages will be prepared in manuscript.

Place	Date	Hour	Summary of Events and Information	Remarks and references to Appendices
DORMAGEN.	1/7/19.	07.00	18th.Bn.K.R.R.C. moved from MARIENBURG to former billets at WORRINGEN in accordance with orders received 29/6/19.	
	4/7/19.		Warning order received from Light Division for Brigade to be in readiness to relieve 1st.Lowland Brigade at SOLINGEN on 9th inst.	
	6/7/19.		Orders received from Light Division postponing move to SOLINGEN for 24 hours.	
	7/7/19.		Band of 18th.Bn.K.R.R.C. and 4 O.R. of each Battalion in the Brigade proceeded to PARIS in charge of Capt.W.J.Taylor 18th.K.R.R.C. to take part in the Victory March through PARIS.	
	10/7/19.		Two companies 18th.K.R.R.C. moved by Lorry to SOLINGEN area to take over outpost line from 51st.H.L.I.	
	11/7/19.	0800	Remainder of Brigade Group proceeded to SOLINGEN by Train and took over accommodation from 1st. Lowland Brigade.	
SOLINGEN.	21/7/19.		The wearing of the British War Medal ribbon authorised.	
	23/7/19.		Observed as a General Holiday to celebrate Peace. A Monetry grant was obtained from Light Division for provision of extra food for the men of the Brigade.	
	31/7/19.	11.00	Major General G.D.Jeffreys,C.B.,C.M.G.,Commanding the Light Division,inspected the billets of this Brigade and visited 13th.Bn.K.R.R.C. during training.	

Capt.
A/Brigade Major,1st.Light Brigade.

www.ingramcontent.com/pod-product-compliance
Lightning Source LLC
Chambersburg PA
CBHW081512160426

43193CB00014B/2668